Chariots of Archangels

ALSO BY NGOZI OLIVIA OSUOHA

The Transformation Train
Letter to My Unborn
Sensation
Tropical Escape (with Amos O. Ojwang')
Fruits from the Poetry Planet
Poetic Grenade
Whispers of the Biafran Skeleton
Chains
Raindrops
Freeborn
Eclipse of Tides
The Subterfuge
Green Snake on a Green Grass

Chariots of Archangels

hymns by
Ngozi Olivia Osuoha

TREASURE COAST BOOKS

©2019 Ngozi Olivia Osuoha

book design and layout: SpiNDec, Port Saint Lucie, FL
cover image: *Ananiel Brings the Storm*, ©2019 Kris Haggblom

All rights reserved.

No part of this book may be used or reproduced in any manner whatsoever without written permission except in the case of brief quotations embodied in critical articles and reviews. Members of educational institutions and organizations wishing to photocopy any of the work for classroom use, or authors, artists and publishers who would like to obtain permission for any material in the work, should contact the publisher.

Published by Treasure Coast Books
Port Saint Lucie, Florida

ISBN: 978-1-950433-35-3

FIRST EDITION
10 9 8 7 6 5 4 3 2 1

dedication

This hymn book is dedicated to the three most ancient schools in my hometown, the schools that have produced professors, heroes, heroines, great and noble men and women in all fields of life:
Boys Secondary School Nkwerrre
St Augustine's Grammar School, Nkwerrre
And especially to my alma mater
St Catharine's Girls' Secondary School, Nkwerrre.

The Hymn Book was one of the requirements when being enrolled in school those days. These schools taught us mysteries in singing, although we were tender and ignorant to really comprehend those days.

contents

When We Weep 1
When We Stagger in the Deep Flood 2
Rejoice All Ye That Are in Pain 4
We Have a God on High 5
Be Strong Dear Friend 6
There Are Many That Are in Chain 7
Now We Have a Lot to Suffer 8
Sing to the Whole World 9
The Earth Is a Training Ground 10
Wake Up All You That Sleep Now 11
There's a Voice Comes Shouting 12
It Does Not Matter What You Lack 14
I Want to Be Your Best Friend, Jesus 15
Dear Lord, We Have Not Any Hope 16
I See a Land 17
Lord, If You Give Me a New Song 18
Never You at All Be Troubled 19
Define Your Life and Your Purpose 20
Now Is the Time 21
The Devil Cannot Do Little 22
The Church Lives in Big Fear 23
When I Think of Your Love Oh Lord 24
Jesus, I Want to Serve You Most 25
When We See Tears 26
Inside This Dungeon and Hill 27
There Is One Friend in the Whole World 28
Wanting Lord to Live for Thee 30
Climb the Mountain 31
Lord, Be My Friend This Day 32
Jesus, You Are the Only One 33

Oh God Give Us the Strength to Stand 34
Father, the Time When We Must Fail 35
Soldiers, Marching on Bare Feet 36
Friends, I Tell You Do Not Fear 37
Heirs With Me, Hope You Are There 38
Jesus, I Fear I'll Lose 39
The Night Is Lone and Long 40
You Can Live a Good Clean Life 41
O Let My Mouth Be Filled With Praise 42
Please Bless Our Land and Make It Rich 43
In This Dark World We See No Light 44
Now We Gather in Mourning 45
Get Up, Make Haste, Delay Not 46
Hear My Child, Hear Thy Father 47
Father, We Are Tired of This Life 48
Since I Came Into This World 49
I Have Nothing to Give Thee, Lord 50
The Foetus in Its Mother's Womb 51
Asleep O Lord We Move Astray 52
Jesus, in This Our Troubled State 53
Saviour, We Bring Before Thee Praise 54
It Is a Thing of Joy O Lord 55
My God, Thou Made the Whole World 56
Dear Lord, Hear This We Poorly Pray 57
There Is a Friend Who Is so Dear 58
Lord, Watch Over Me When I Sleep 59
We Have Some Friends Who Sell Us Cheap 60
Abide Lord With Those in Sickbed 61
Keep Not Thy Blessing Lord on Hold 62
We Move from Place to Place in Life 63

Chariots of Archangels

1. When We Weep
to the tune of: LORD, THY WORD ABIDETH

When we weep like infant
In the face of deep despair
God will rise like elephant
And make us free and fair.

When we plant and sow and sow
Hoping to reap in harvest
With the foe crushing us low
Then our God will bring the best.

He can come like a good friend
Just to bring us down beneath
But our God sits at the end
So we shall not see death.

Though the world is very dark
Our God shall be then our light,
For we bear on us His mark
He shall give us His might.

We wait for the last day
When God shall give us a kiss
We yearn for that great repay
It shall be just a bliss.

2. When We Stagger in the Deep Flood
to the tune of: ALLELUIA, SING TO JESUS

When we stagger in the deep flood
The foe thinks he has won it
As we lay cold like log of wood
He believes his target is hit
Then our God descends from on high
Causing His people to shout
Turning every grief and sigh
Into joy to shame the tout.

Like the night that wakes a new morn
Bitterness is dark and red
All the pain that brings the new born
Labour is too good and bad
But our God has healed our wounds
And made His chosen people dance
'Cause our gladness knows no bounds
Thank you Lord for this great chance.

We know that the foe may come back
But we are never afraid
Though he wears the face of great lack
Jesus bought and stored and paid
Till the end we can't exhaust all
That our God has stored for us
Life, wealth, food, cloth and high wall
And all the total bonus.

If we hang on just a moment
No matter what we go through
If we want a new improvement

It can come with great breakthrough,
So no fear can make us doubt God
Because He'll provide for us
This our God rules the whole world
And He is our dear locus.

3. Rejoice All Ye That Are in Pain
to the tune of: HOW SWEET THE NAME OF JESUS SOUNDS

Rejoice all ye that are in pain
For soon our King shall come
And this shall be our glorious gain
To be with Him at home.

Never let your hands grow weary
Nor let your legs cripple
Let nothing make you feel dreary
The world needs that nipple.

Let every tear roll down with joy
No matter the harshness
Your God is not a little boy
He knows your bitterness.

Until you give your very best
You have never given,
Forget the terrors of the past
There is a new heaven.

The world we live in is not ours
It is old and decayed
But heaven is not theirs but ours
It will not be delayed.

4. We Have a God on High
to the tune of: LORD JESUS, THINK ON ME

We have a God on high
He sees through our whole heart
He reads the pain and writes the sighs
And masters all the art.

When we slumber and faint
He holds us by the hand
And makes each one of us a saint
And recovers His land.

Just a little raindrop
That's enough for His work,
He would not let anyone flop
He prunes His vine with fork.

Jesus, you love us much
But we love you just small,
Please let us love you well and such
And cause us not to fall.

Jesus, the only food
Let us unite and eat,
Humble your people as we stoop
As this is a retreat.

5. Be Strong Dear Friend
to the tune of: IMMORTAL LOVE FOREVER FLOW

Be strong dear friend and never frown
Arise and work with zeal,
For God is coming with your crown
And He has made your meal.

Move on poor friend and be joyous
The pain, the shame, the hunger
Push them aside, be ye conscious
For they all won't linger.

Before us comes the lightning wave
Flying like a speed boat
Behind us is the deepest grave
But God is near afloat.

Stand up, step out, begin your day
Your work is less than grace
Though you are nothing but some clay
Your shield knows no disgrace.

The world is rough and soiled and wild
And has no place for goodness
But Him you serve is soft and mild
And knows no bitterness.

6. There Are Many That Are in Chain
to the tune of: GOD MOVES IN A MYSTERIOUS WAY

There are many that are in chain
They know not even so
As they see it as their own gain
They know nothing to do.

These ones can work better for God
Only if they are freed
So Lord destroy the chain with rod
And make them your own seed.

Some of your lands are dark and dead
Thick darkness covers all,
Please Lord descend and give them bread
And let them stand up tall.

The few that are too small and short
Are fighting with weakness
They wail and weep as they get hurt
Dear Lord, send them richness.

Let all the earth be made to hear
That the Lord is her king
And let none have nothing to fear
Rather a hymn to sing.

7. Now We Have a Lot to Suffer
to the tune of: FATHER, HEAR THE PRAYER WE OFFER

Now we have a lot to suffer
Because we are in the world
Soon we shall rejoice and offer
As we lay down every sword.

Today the war is very tight
Making the called to look back
Putting some to run and to flight
But our God has patched the crack.

No matter the Satan's weapon
He cannot conquer God's fold,
On and on, we all shall march on
For our God has made us bold.

In the morning we still fight him
In the noon we shall not sleep,
In the night we fight and sing hymn
We must make the foe to weep.

Lord help us in this great battle
Let your grace wake all the dead
Feed and shelter all the cattle
Till the crown is on our head.

8. Sing to the Whole World
to the tune of: HARK! HARK! MY SOUL, ANGELIC SONGS ARE SWELLING

Sing, sing, my mouth, for God has opened my lips
Sing oh my soul, do not be cold or dead,
For God has healed my breasts and troubled hips
Awake my soul and raise up tall your head.
Chorus:
Sing to the whole world, sing to the north
Sing to the east and west and then to the south.

Sing oh sing on, the devil must be ashamed
Sing on and dance let the earth hear your voice
The day of God is here, he cannot be blamed
This is the day Jesus long paid the price.
Chorus:

The bitterness inside the dirty gutter
Is not up to the blessings that abound
Look around you there is a soothing butter
It is there to see more in the muddy ground.
Chorus:

Take heed to stand up each time you fall down
Let nothing keep you there over awhile,
Jesus had washed so white your dirty gown
It is so new just like that other new file.
Chorus:

Though in the world, we live as strangers down here
That's why we pay even through our noses
A day shall come, when we shall retire up there
And the chapter and page of this world closes.
Chorus:

9. The Earth Is a Training Ground
to the tune of: SONGS OF PRAISE, THE ANGELS SING

The earth is a training ground
So learn well from each mistake
Let all the treasures be found
This is why you have a stake.

The strife may be just a game
God and Satan made a bet
Though none knows your little fame
Hold on, keep on, don't be wet.

Life is cruel and sometimes strange
Bringing down the good and poor
Causing him to back the change
And shut himself out the door.

Let the called arise and shine
March on serpents and scorpions
God promised we would be fine
He gave us much more onions.

Let us all renew our thought
As God cleans our dirty mind
He will give us all we sought
As He comes from our behind.

10. Wake Up All You That Sleep Now
to the tune of: STAND UP, STAND UP FOR JESUS

Wake up all you that sleep now
The foe is coming near
He is approaching with no fear
Come on, let's milk this cow,
Our God has given us the grace
To look him in the face
And fight him at the same pace
To win the glorious race.

Help him that's brokenhearted
Tell him our God is good
Give him the sweet Jesus' food
His heart will be melted,
Help him, help him, help each one
Mostly those who are so lone
Bind them and strengthen their bone
And all would form a cone.

As you live in this rough time
Beware you can slip off
So let the Lord be your gulf
This is a sure defence,
Then only then you are sure
If not there is not one cure
But God will make you all pure
And you will be so sure.

11. There's a Voice Comes Shouting
to the tune of: THERE'S A CALL COMES RINGING O'ER THE RESTLESS WAVE

There's a voice comes shouting o'er the hurricane
Heal the land, heal the land
There's a child comes running 'round the crash-ed plane
Heal the land, heal the land.
Heal the land, this poor terrible land
Make it good and rich again,
Heal the land, this miserable dead land
Let us sow and reap again.

In the day, we work as if we are just slaves
Heal the land, heal the land
In the night, we sleep like beasts in those small caves
Heal this land, heal this land.
Heal the land, this dirty troubled land
Make it nice and free again
Heal the land, this horrible old land
Show us love and peace again.

We die at the top of our good work
Heal the land, heal the land
We till and scatter and clean up our fork
Heal the land, heal the land
Heal the land! This thorny wicked land
Let us till and sow our crops
Heal the land! This bitter swampy land
Bless the dew and the raindrops.

Heal the land and let the beasts live together
Heal the land, heal this land

Heal this land and let the waters be just there
Heal the land, heal the land.
Heal the land! This shady-shaky land
Let the wars and the crimes be ceased
Heal the land, this sloppy-bumpy land
Let thy peace and grace be increased.

12. It Does Not Matter What You Lack
to the tune of: HOW SWEET THE NAME OF JESUS SOUNDS

It does not matter what you lack
The Lord is there to fill
Just make sure you don't turn your back
From Him who pays the bill.

The problem that keeps you awake
Hides itself from our God
Because he works now for your sake
Smiting fears with his rod.

Tomorrow shall be bright and good
For thus the Lord has said
So let that be your soul's rich food
The Lord has even paid.

Whether you lie on dirty rug
Whether you sleep on mat
Whether you wake with bites of bug
Whether you eat just rat.

You have so great amazing gift
Just look up to heaven
And make sure your legs do not shift
Let the bread not leaven.

13. I Want to Be Your Best Friend, Jesus
to the tune of: PASS ME NOT O GENTLE SAVIOUR

I want to be your best friend, Jesus
Come into my heart
Let nothing make me lose my focus
Even when I'm fat
My friend, my friend, Jesus you are my best friend
Though I faint and fall and tire and stop
Lead me to the end.

I see things that force me to give up
They are close and near
Jesus help me also with this cup
Lift me up to bear.
My priest, my priest, Jesus you are my high priest
Though I crawl or walk or run or fly
Prepare thou, my feast.

Let me live with you in the same room
For me to be neat
Then you would be my only bridegroom
Knowing how to treat.
My love, my love, Jesus you are my own love
When I am asleep or down or dead
You will make me move.

Above all my lord for thee I wait
Though you come too late
I know you can put all things so straight
Even the steel gate.
My lord, my lord, Jesus you are my dear Lord
Cause me to be still and calm and cool
Though I see discord.

14. Dear Lord, We Have Not Any Hope
to the tune of: O JESUS, I HAVE PROMISED

Dear Lord, we have not any hope
For they are set to kill
We have been tied with a long rope
Waiting to roll from the hill
So lord come now, come speedily
Cut the rope, set us free
Come Lord rescue the needy
And make name just for thee.

We look up, down and around
Hearing no sound , no voice
Those who want us inside the ground
Have vowed there is no choice,
But lo, thou art the only one
Who can vow and fulfill
So lord vow and it be done
Lest they eat from our skull.

Oh lord these chains are heavy
Break them and let us go
Make us thy divine army
Declare and make it so
Oh Jesus let the whole world hear
That now we are thy troop
Hold us and let nothing us fear
For we are in thy group.

15. I See a Land
to the tune of: MY HOPE IS BUILT ON NOTHING LESS

I see a land that flows with milk
As I wear my fine golden silk
Dancing around the tallest wall
Harping with joy the altar call,
It has also the sweet honey
Which cannot be bought with money
Come and taste it and be nourished.

I hear a voice that calls us all
Even after the great nightfall
It says my wandering children, come
I built for you a golden home
There is nothing like death nor strife
Nor anyone that kills with knife
Come and live there and be nourished.

I feel a hand that gives us warmth
Withdraw from His amazing wrath
He guides our soul around the field
Guarding us too with His strong shield.
The lord our God is here within
Let everyone desist from sin
Hear and obey and be nourished.

16. Lord, If You Give Me a New Song
to the tune of: MY HOPE IS BUILT ON NOTHING LESS

Lord, if you give me a new song
I will sing it for very long
Lord, if you change my bad story
I will shout for that victory.
So unto you lord, now I cry
Let not my voice wear out and dry
Please grant me all these I pray now.

You died on the cross for my sin
To help me stand tall the world; win
Yet I fight with my little faith
When you have died for me my death,
Lord, please hold me by your own hand
And lead me through this dirty land
Lord, I beg you to be with me.

If your hand holds me firm and tight
I shall win then all the fight
If your grace seals me from the rear
I shall maintain your holy gear,
On you lord, I relax
Let every fear melt down like wax
Then I shall be your true warrior.

17. Never You at All Be Troubled
to the tune of: HOW SWEET THE NAME OF JESUS SOUNDS

Never you at all be troubled
Nor let your strength grow faint
Because your grace is now doubled
As in the days; ancient.

Let nothing make you lose your grip
The lord shall not delay
Instead tell that coin not to flip
The lord does not mean play.

As we gather under this tent
And wait to carry on
The foe is asking for some rent
Despite our God has won.

Omnipotent is our dear king
Our God who reigns supreme
Omnipresent is He in ring
He fights to the extreme.

Try Him and prove all His wonders
Tell them that seek a proof
Our God echoes in the thunders
He mounts above the roof.

18. Define Your Life and Your Purpose
to the tune of: HOW SWEET THE NAME OF JESUS SOUNDS

Define your life and your purpose
Do not yet seek repose
Give yourself that authentic name
That God called when you came.

Many have died without a mark
Many are in the dark
And they abound without a trace
That fainted on the race.

Waiting for fish and bread divine
Takes no one through the vine
Instead work out your salvation
And live in God's nation.

Stand up and walk through the garden
And less now your burden
So shall your load reduce and drop
Then you can pluck some crop.

This world we dwell in is not safe
Around is flying knife,
So cover yourself under God
Let Him be your Concord.

19. Now Is the Time
to the tune of: WHILE SHEPHERDS WATCHED THEIR FLOCKS BY NIGHT

Now is the time, come and drink from
The water for the earth
For your life to have a reform
So that you won't see death.

This day you have the grace to see
So make broad your vision
Let nothing stop you to be free
Arise, stay on mission.

There is an angel with you now
Tearing down all the wall
Step in and never ask him how
He will not let you fall.

Your chance is sure but do not fear
For God is on your side
He is the greatest shield you bear
Arise and beat the tide.

The dead and living hear His voice
Without Him speaking twice
Listen and live and fear His hand
He can smite a whole land.

20. The Devil Cannot Do Little
to the tune of: HOW SWEET THE NAME OF JESUS SOUNDS

The devil cannot do little
So let him go his way
He lost the old and new battle
He has nowhere to stay.

Beyond the flesh he's defeated
We must not let him in
Let nobody have us cheated
We are costlier than tin.

Banish him far to the desert
Let him dwell there alone
By that you do, a lot avert
Even if he dares clone.

Now let us fear God like David
And sing Him glorious psalms
Then we shall see Him so vivid
Inscribe us on His palms.

Keep not your arrows in quiver
Sleep not, rest not, stand firm
Jug on with no more cold liver
God will surely affirm.

21. The Church Lives in Big Fear
to the tune of: MY SPIRIT LONGS FOR THEE

The church lives in big fear
Marching on through the year
Yet still in deep anguish
Lord, please let her flourish.

The church goes on like that
Growing lean-fat fat-lean
Lord, make her growth steady
And too fully ready.

The church meets up and down
Boldly shown in her frown,
By the next agony
She may too grow thorny.

Lord, let your hand arise
Let there be a sunrise
Speak to the worlds apart
To put aright the chart.

The past saints saw your face
They completed their race
Lord, show us your mercy
In this our regency.

22. When I Think of Your Love Oh Lord
to the tune of: MY GOD HOW WONDERFUL THOU ART

When I think of your love oh lord
I feel like just a child
That you feed me with your fresh word
And make me young and mild.

The storms of life push me too far
And make me to look back
Yet you help me to shine like star
And shield me from my lack.

When I get weak and dying sick
You come on my sickbed
Saying to me I made your brick
Only you I did wed.

Rough paths are here and there, all round
But I know you are near
The foe wants me to roll on ground
But I am to you, dear.

Father, Son, Holy ghost, three one
I hope I am stainless
Before you come, please be it done
Join me in your oneness.

23. Jesus, I Want to Serve You Most
to the tune of: MY GOD HOW WONDERFUL THOU ART

Jesus, I want to serve you most
Please be my strength and host,
So that I shall put in my best
And then come up to rest.

You said up there is beautiful
The sights are wonderful,
So cause me lord to be your friend
And rest after the bend.

There is no matter so crucial
No place can be special,
That under your own government
It shall be wonderment.

Bind everything that does distract
Keep us firm, strong, intact
Let nothing come our dwelling place
Instead show us your face.

Jesus, now, then, today, morrow
May we see no sorrow
Defend our foundation and edge
Without our own knowledge.

24. When We See Tears
to the tune of: GI ATULA EGWU

When we see tears and fears
Our faith then quake and shake
The foe so tickles and twinkles
And we dress back and back.

When we face want and pant
We grumble and stumble
Still it makes God no boy nor toy
Because He sees the bees.

From to the past to the last
From ages to ages
God has been there our hope and scope
Let nothing beat or cheat.

They may come sour and raw
And make your blood to flood
For them to have their drink and wink
Look not the tide to hide.

Now you must talk and walk
Also sing in the ring
Else too they think they win your chin
Knowing not you get set.

25. Inside This Dungeon and Hill
to the tune of: LORD, IN THIS THY MERCY'S DAY

Inside this dungeon and hill
There is someone near to kill,
Jesus, come and pay my bill.

Around here we all do smell
Even where we built to dwell
Jesus, come and bless this well.

When we sow, we wait to reap
Praying that we make a heap,
In the end they crash so cheap.

Lord, arise, address this shame
Spread abroad your work and fame
Let the earth bow at your name.

Then the end, both old and young
Then the prize, both weak and strong
Then the joy, both now and long.

Lift us up to cross the stream
Fill us up with holy dream
Tie us all as one great team.

26. There Is One Friend in the Whole World
to the tune of: WHAT A FRIEND WE HAVE IN JESUS

There is one friend in the whole world
He is everywhere you go
You can see him when you need him
He is such a true dear friend.
When you need some whispers in your ear
You will get as much you pray
Because you will hear him so clear
That is just the course to stay.

There is one unique big brother
He lights up the way for us
He goes first to conquer the end
So that we shall come unhurt.
There is no more fear along the road
He cleared it and made it straight,
By the sides he dropped every load
And we have nothing to wait.

There is just one only guardian
What an expert in guidance
Follow him and land in heaven
You will never regret it.
When the beast comes up like a deep flood
He will stop and wage and calm
It can never be in vain, his blood
For it is also our balm.

There is one lord in the universe
He is king of kings also
He was there before the whole world

You are on right track with him.
Look, not back, keep on, just face your front
This lord will see you all through
All those matters, He shall confront
You will wonder if it's you.

27. Wanting Lord to Live for Thee
to the tune of: LORD, IN THIS THY MERCY'S DAY

Wanting lord to live for thee
Panting lord to hear thy voice,
Planting lord to reap from thee.

Longing, friend, that I may know
Singing, friend, to show thy praise
Shouting, friend, to tell thy works.

Hungering for thy touch once more
Thirsting for thy smile right now,
Hoping for thy light on me.

Wondering why the world is mad
Pondering why the earth is dead,
Thundering why no one endures.

Going up and down is vain
Moving back and forth is fake,
Rolling left and right is waste.

Tearing the mask now I do
Fearing nothing on the way,
Nearing Jesus at all cost.

28. Climb the Mountain
to the tune of: GI ATULA EGWU

Climb the mountain and sound
Ring the bell right from there
Tell the world, she is no more bound
That her own lord is here.

Gather the sons of men
Teach them the way to go
Let them write down with their own pen
That the lord God said so.

Let everyone labour
And see that he is strong
Let every man help his neighbour
The journey may be long.

The great can fall as well
The small can be too big
So let all fight and banish hell
Learn also from that fig.

29. Lord, Be My Friend This Day
to the tune of: GI ATULA EGWU

Lord, be my friend this day
Show me the long best track
And help me not to slip away,
Father, stand at my back.

When the night is too long
Help me to keep awake
Touch my soul and let me be strong
Please for your kingdom's sake.

During the strange famine
Feed me and your household
Open our eyes to see the mine
Which you keep for your fold.

Bring in all those you called
Seal them with your own mark
And lead them through where you have walked
Though those evil dogs bark.

30. Jesus, You Are the Only One
to the tune of: O GOD OUR HELP IN AGES PAST

Jesus, you are the only one
That truly knows our pain
You were here then, now you are gone
It means we can be plain.

Jesus, they blackmailed you on earth
And lied that you blasphemed
Spat at you, flogged you, put to death
King of the Jews "nicknamed"

Jesus, you fed the poorest poor
And freed the captive man
You broke the gate and the strong door
And lifted all the ban.

Jesus, you saw the bad grow worse
You saw the good decay
Please teach the world your holy course
And spread your hopeful ray.

Jesus, we come, oh let us know
That you are here with us
Bind all that makes us not to show
That you are our focus.

Jesus, when they burn us like coal
Help us to stand so tall,
Give us the zeal to reach the goal
And never ever fall.

31. Oh God Give Us the Strength to Stand
to the tune of: O GOD OUR HELP IN AGES PAST

Oh God give us the strength to stand
And fight the foe to still
Renew this weak and troubled band
Mount us on the top hill.

Dear lord the track is dark and long
We want to see clearer
So let your angels raise a song
That would draw us nearer.

Dear lord, this call is rough and tough
Please let us enjoy it
Guide us and that will be enough
For us to cross the pit.

Dear lord remember your promise
That you will be with us,
Please let us never compromise
The shame, the pain, the cross.

When we are down with confusion
Be near to help us think
Let us not draw a conclusion
That we are made to sink.

32. Father, the Time When We Must Fail
to the tune of: O GOD OUR HELP IN AGES PAST

Father, the time when we must fail
Touch us to read the mail,
So that we will learn from the trash
And never again crash.

Jesus, when we have lost it all
Draw near and help us hear
That you have for us a great call
And that we are so dear.

Spirit, chase far those who oppose
Your work and reign in us
Pursue them far and never close
And bless our dream's locus.

O God, three in one, one in three
The earth and hell are yours
We beg thee make us always free
And take all the honours.

33. Soldiers, Marching on Bare Feet
to the tune of: CHRISTIAN, SEEK NOT YET REPOSE

Soldiers, marching on bare feet
Beware that the thorns have root
Make sure you put on your boot,
   March with strength.

Soldiers, looking front and back
Beware, you don't have to slack
Lighten all things in your sack,
   Don't give up.

Soldiers, know deep who you are
Take heed and also take care
That the foe does not you dare,
   Stand up tall.

Soldiers, your captain is strong
Fight on no matter how long,
With him nothing shall go wrong,
   Hang on there!

Soldiers, hiding from front line
You will lose your big goldmine
Stand up, dust yourselves, be fine;
   For the crown.

34. Friends, I Tell You Do Not Fear
to the tune of: CHRISTIAN, SEEK NOT YET REPOSE

Friends, I tell you do not fear
You have all it takes to win
I give you new grace each day
  I am near.

Friends, I wish that you would live
That was why I came and died
So that you would have full life,
  Friends, believe!

Friends, my palms were pierced for you
Touch them now and feel the hole
It was too painful to bear,
  I bore it!

Friends, my lungs were pierced for all
Touch them now and feel the hole
Arrows passed through my body,
  For you all.

Friends, my feet were pierced for you
They were nailed upon the tree
My head also crowned with thorns,
  Just for you!

Friends, believe me I did all
Because you were near the grave,
So I came for your rescue;
  Friends, please live!

35. Heirs With Me, Hope You Are There
to the tune of: CHRISTIAN, SEEK NOT YET REPOSE

Heirs with me, hope you are there
Soon, there will be great rapture
Be sure you are on your guard
  Time is near!

Heirs with me, be counting down
There will be no more delay
Stay firm on your duty post,
   Time is near!

Heirs with me, forget the world
There is nothing, good in it
What you have coming is great,
  Time is near!

Heirs with me, do not fail me
I have made all things so new
Guard your heart with these my words,
   Time is near!

Heirs with me, don't be deceived
The foe wears a rope that shines,
Transforming into a light;
God's not mocked!

36. Jesus, I Fear I'll Lose
to the tune of: THY WAY NOT MINE, O LORD

Jesus, I fear I'll lose
Because I see danger
Teach me the winning life
And make me no stranger.

Jesus, I dread the storm
I don't like any wave,
Wake up and calm the sea
Only you are that brave.

Jesus, I hate this world
That's why it takes me deep
Because I shall go up
When I fall down asleep.

Jesus, I want to come
Wrap me in your safe arm
Kiss me and bless my head
So that I meet no harm.

Jesus, cut short the fight
Let our freedom begin,
Lose the bonds and tear the mask
That were engrossed in sin.

37. The Night Is Lone and Long
to the tune of: THY WAY NOT MINE, O LORD

The night is lone and long
With no food nor water
The night is soaked and slow
Where will all the pain flow?

The day is bored and brief
With no friend, no brother
The day is hard and tough
The people look so rough.

The world is old and gone
With nothing sweet or new
The world; broken and spent
This is the truth not bent.

This life is blurred and fake
With everything so odd
This life is cruel and harsh
That's why we all can crash.

But Lord, you know us all
You made each of our frame
Dear lord you know our make
Touch us to be awake.

Dear lord, please make us new
Breathe on us life and strength
Clean up this world our God
Make it your Paradise.

38. You Can Live a Good Clean Life
to the tune of: ALL THINGS BRIGHT AND BEAUTIFUL

You can live a good clean life
You can love your neighbour
You can even feed the poor
Yet you will be hated.

Chorus:
Move on, God is watching
Move on and not look back,
Move on, there is a God
Who cometh with your prize.

You can build a church for God
You can serve Him to end
You can pay all your tithes well
Yet you will have troubles.

You can watch all things you say
You may never tell lies
You may not live in their midst
Yet they will butcher you.

You try to keep all the rules
You struggle to keep peace
You will pray always for all
Yet they will not like you.

39. O Let My Mouth Be Filled With Praise
to the tune of: BE THOU MY GUARDIAN

O let my mouth be filled with praise
That I may serve my king
Withhold the forces that me oppose
And give me a new song.

Teach me to fast and watch and pray
So I can fight the foe
Help me to strike him down the way
Before he grabs my toe.

The war, the fight and the battle
Are fierce and stern and raw
So lord, throw down thy great mantle
That we may break its jaw.

Draw near to us oh lord we seek
And hold us by the hand
Pursue the beast and not the meek
Give them, O lord, the land.

From not my God on us poor sinners
Recall we are mere flesh
Instead transform and make us winners
Recreate us lord afresh.

40. Please Bless Our Land and Make It Rich
to the tune of: HOW SWEET THE NAME OF JESUS SOUNDS

Please bless our land and make it rich
So that we would be glad
O fertilize our crop by inch
And make the tare so sad.

Bless then our time through every sweat
And flourish all our seed
May those who laugh and on us cheat
See us blossom in feed.

As we pray for thy heavenly rain
Never fail to give shine,
Let all our sorrows turn to gain
Because you give us wine.

In torture, torment, hurricane
Be thou our duty post
In shame, dishonour, and in sane
Remain our goal utmost.

When troubles knock on every door
Be dear our guide and guard
When we fall deep down and go poor
Be near us to safeguard.

41. In This Dark World We See No Light
to the tune of: WHEN ALL THY MERCIES O MY GOD

In this dark world we see no light
No friend really does care
We run helter-skelter in pain
And dash our feet in blight.

In this lonely troubled jungle
No one is there for you,
We run up, down, left, right, centre
And yet live in struggle.

In this valley of great stronghold
Nothing is done that fine,
No one is near, no one is dear
You are just there so cold.

In this pit of abounding fear
Love is nowhere around
Hate is here and hate is still there
Your eyes know every tear.

Countless violence is everywhere
Countless rape is just here
Countless problems within, without
Yet countless joy up there.

42. Now We Gather in Mourning
to the tune of: OFT IN DANGER OFT IN WOE

Now we gather in mourning
Weeping like a new baby
Soon shall come our peace divine
Not too long we shall be fine.

Now we come in great weakness
Struggling to lift up our eyes
Soon our strength shall be kindled
And our pain shall be humbled.

Brethren, hold strong all your hands
The band of our foes shall see,
Let not their echo scare you
Here comes now the big breakthrough.

The chosen of God be wise
Lean not on whate'er you hear
Put back hardship and trials
You will reap all denials.

Remember, we are soldiers
Weep no more and stand up tall
Let your sword never be down
See up there has sent your crown.

43. Get Up, Make Haste, Delay Not
to the tune of: OFT IN DANGER OFT IN WOE

Get up, make haste, delay not
Tear off all dirty garment,
Run, meet the foe at the front
Make haste dear, your bold movement.

Rise up, forget bread and wine
Those are just food to the flesh
Speed up your flight and get there
Your strength shall be made afresh.

Do not whisper to the world
Hence they hitch your moving train
Move, your God is by your side
Catch up, do not bear a stain.

The world is heartless and cruel
Felling down those on their course
See that you have no hindrance
Not even one inter-course

Listen, hearken and obey
You would be glad that you did
Save yourself from senseless group
This advice is too candid.

44. Hear My Child, Hear Thy Father
to the tune of: LORD, IN THIS THY MERCY'S DAY

Hear my child, hear thy father
Hear thy lord, and thy maker
Hear and live, there is danger.

In this world, there is evil
Everything; stained by devil
E'en the ones looking; weevil.

He planted time bomb under
Making all look like wonder
He is here pleading thunder.

There is none beside me; son
Come home and you have him won
Come my son, I love you son.

You have failed and failed again
You have gone and gone in pain
Come home son and make good gain.

I will count your sin no more
I will make you cross the shore,
Come home son and be at fore.

45. Father, We Are Tired of This Life
to the tune of: FATHER HEAR THE PRAYER WE OFFER

Father, we are tired of this life
Cut asunder with thy knife
Everything the foe has stolen
Let the hard chain be broken.

Father, now we long to be free
Let us flourish like the tree
Water us from thy holy throne
Let us rise again like bone.

We come, father, accept us now
Please cleanse us by anyhow
Keep us near the blood of Jesus
Keep us clean, neat like Jesus.

We are tired of all the scorning
We are fed up with mourning
Nothing here is evermore sweet
Lord, accept, accept, we meet.

For the sake of our foe, arise
Thou the best, purest and wise
Arise, lord, arise and save us
Thou art all and all our cross.

46. Since I Came Into This World
to the tune of: SOME HAVE FOOD BUT CANNOT EAT

Since I came into this world
I have known no happiness
All I see is shame and blame
Jesus, lord, come now to save.

Since I came into this world
Troubles chase me like shadow
All I hear is game and lame
Jesus, lord, quicken thy help.

Since I was a child till now
War and trauma rule the day
All I dream is fear and tear
Jesus, lord, speed up thy flight.

Since I knew to write my name
Echoes faint the calls I get
All I feel is wear from tear
Jesus, lord, call me to serve.

Since I grew into a man
Violence rules the world I know
All I grab is lock and knock
Jesus, lord, put up thy fight.

Since I claimed to be of age
Nothing good I can boast of
All I pray is rock and shock
Jesus, lord, arise and shine.

47. I Have Nothing to Give Thee, Lord
to the tune of: HOW SWEET THE NAME OF JESUS SOUNDS

I have nothing to give thee lord
Please let my prayer count
Be near to rule and direct me
In times of confusion.

I know nothing to tell the world
O lord, speak through my mouth
Let each word of mine be by grace
To those who need it most.

I am not a saint nor angel
But let thy spirit grow
Cause every word that cometh forth
To germinate and spread.

Thou chooseth whom thou lovest lord
Thou chooseth not by fame
 Thou chooseth not by credentials
Instead by thy order.

If thou base it just by merit
No one could work for thee
That's why thou make it by mercy
And choose those thou chooseth.

48. The Foetus in Its Mother's Womb
to the tune of: HOW SWEET THE NAME OF JESUS SOUNDS

The foetus in its mother's womb
O lord, preserve and keep
Hatch it, grow it, O bring it forth
May it never see tomb.

In due time, may we gather lord
To bless and share in joy
As we lay him in front of thee
To help fight this dark world.

He shall be red hot on the foe
And he must win through thee
His mission must not be cut short
Until the vanquished, foe.

In all he does, he'll know no Ill
For thou shall be his zeal
His love, his faith, his hope, his all
His foundation, thy will.

Help him when confusion appears
Hide him through the coarse voice
Separate the tare, the weed, the grain
Till the foe disappears.

49. Asleep O Lord We Move Astray
to the tune of: HOW SWEET THE NAME OF JESUS SOUNDS

Asleep O lord we move astray
We dwell above our sense
And there nothing we know at all
Then the foe can betray.

In dream we see things wild, absurd
We fight to come back home
And then forces on us let loose
Unless thou solve the surd.

We battle when we close our eyes
All life gone, lying dead
If thou delay to wake us up
We are gone in our eyes.

Midnight, woke up by dreadful dream
We dare not sleep again
Our bed, our room, and our partner
All become horror stream.

Alone, thou art the one to keep
Thou too can take away
Thou can pour on us thy true peace
And cause our foes to sleep.

50. Jesus, in This Our Troubled State
to the tune of: HOW SWEET THE NAME OF JESUS SOUNDS

Jesus, in this our troubled state
Do not tarry to come
Our eyes are fainting, growing weak
Please come, dear lord, our date.

We cry out all our tears at once
Hoping to solve the case
The more we wail, the more the pain
Come Jesus, our substance.

We pant and jump up in trauma
Wishing it happened not
Forcing ourselves to wake from dream
Praying, the end; drama.

The truth be told, it is bitter
No matter who is wrong
Innocent, spotless, clean and green;
Even the bomb-letter.

Safe beneath thy wings we draw near
Keep us evermore there
Let nothing pluck us from thy hand
Nor fill our heart with fear.

51. Saviour, We Bring Before Thee Praise
to the tune of: HOW SWEET THE NAME OF JESUS SOUNDS

Saviour, we bring before thee praise
We thank thee for thy might
Dead, we would have been long ago
If thou had not saved us.

Saviour, we fall on thy feet now
Receive our Thanksgiving,
We watched and got lost how we won
Dear lord, thank you again.

Lord, thou chose to save thy people
And bless thy heritage
Thou passed over our foes by night
And made them weep by day.

Lord, thou did tear our mourning clothes
Gave us a new garment
Thou wrapped us in peace and glory
And bid us rest divine.

Jesus, the son of God most high
Who can call thee to fight,
When the world powers worship thee
And pray thee for thy strength?

52. It Is a Thing of Joy O Lord
to the tune of: HOW SWEET THE NAME OF JESUS SOUNDS

It is a thing of joy O lord
That thou came to save us
We would have been in deep darkness
If thou kept mute above.

Thy mercy, compassion and love
Thou came to pour on us
E'en when we wangle in valley
Thou came right there for us.

Thy favour, vision and calmness
Thou brought upon our bone
E'en in the tunnel of danger
Thou rescued us from sin.

Thy peace, guidance and protection
Thou shared on our poor souls
In firmness of divinity
Thou brought us joy untold.

We cannot thank thee well enough
No matter what we give
We cannot do it right and right
Because we are humans.

53. My God, Thou Made the Whole World
to the tune of: OFT IN DANGER OFT IN WOE

My God, thou made the whole world
Thou didst know the bounding lines
Help us to not cross the banks
Thou know all our shortcomings.

My God thou who gave us life
Thou didst know how long we'll live
Teach us to live by thy word
Let us know our days ahead.

My God if we fail to pray
Quicken the gift thou didst give,
Water the zeal in our heart
May we grow the way thou choose.

Our God, build thy wall o'er us
Lest we lose the side of peace
Our God hold our hands and help
That we may not fail nor fall.

54. Dear Lord, Hear This We Poorly Pray
to the tune of: HOW SWEET THE NAME OF JESUS SOUNDS

Dear lord, hear this we poorly pray
Make haste and not delay
Descend with all thy strength and might
And put the foe to flight.

When he plans to keep us in dark
Letting his dogs to bark
Cause him to lose every battle
And safeguard thy cattle.

When he paints us with black and red
Staining with blood, our bed
Stand tall, look upon Jesus blood
To back and cease the flood.

He sings lies and threats on the street
He shares blackmails on sheet
He declares wars and treachery
Lord, make him a mockery.

His vows are bad and mischievous
His passion is dangerous
His intent is only deceit
Nothing but counterfeit.

Dear lord, arise and shine on earth
Breathe on us thy own breath
Cause the devil to run and run
And always on the run.

55. There Is a Friend Who Is so Dear
to the tune of: HOW SWEET THE NAME OF JESUS SOUNDS

There is a friend who is so dear
He is near and around
There is nothing again to fear
He is always on ground.

This friend cares so much about us
He understands our fear
He draws us to the true focus
And buries all our fears.

When life lashes on us its worst
And rolls us on the mud
This friend does not allow us burst
Rather waters our bud.

There is one thing he dares not do
Be it the worst sinner,
He would not let him die and go
Because he made dinner.

This friend is faithful, timely and just
Even in time of pain
He knows we are nothing but dust
So he helps us make gain.

Come to Him now ye dead and gone
Come to him, slave of sin
Come back home he will pursue none
Come you will lose no pin.

56. Lord, Watch Over Me When I Sleep
to the tune of: HOW SWEET THE NAME OF JESUS SOUNDS

Lord, watch over me when I sleep
Mostly when I go deep
My bed, my room, my house, my world
Let them obey thy word.

Some people made themselves my foes
Some others want my toes
I may not know they do exist,
To save me lord, insist.

The world of dream is life and death
Opposite of the earth
One can lie down to sleep and die
With no trace to the pie.

So lord we pray thee watch us close
The foe must surely lose
Draw the line that he cannot cross
Tell him you are the boss.

Jesus sometimes we dream away
And we forget the day
Believing we are dead and gone
Until thou touch our bone.

Jesus those who live on the night
Force us to weigh thy might,
Jesus teach them to keep thy law
Or have thy wrath too raw.

57. We Have Some Friends Who Sell Us Cheap
to the tune of: HOW SWEET THE NAME OF JESUS SOUNDS

We have some friends who sell us cheap
We have brothers that kill
These ones gather us in a heap
And do whate'er they will.

There are fathers that kill daughters
Mothers that bury sons
To them nothing at all matters
They depend on their guns.

Children do not obey parents
Family; a war front
They raze down their own very tents
Whether or not palm front.

The world at large is in deep mess
Nothing is in good shape
The world is gone, worn out, in stress
Falling, falling to rape.

Yet all these happen, no one cares
None longs to see a change
Satan weakens all those in prayers
Making all things too strange.

Arise O lord, O lord arise
Thine is the might to heal
Arise, arise, arise, arise
Arise, O lord to heal.

58. Abide Lord With Those in Sickbed
to the tune of: HOW SWEET THE NAME OF JESUS SOUNDS

Abide lord with those in sickbed
Let them thy grace receive
Recall the blood for them was shed
Cause them no more to grieve.

Lord, some widows eat their own flesh
Because they have no hope
Please lord release on them love fresh
Help them to live and cope.

Abide lord with all those orphans
Wherever they may be
Cause them to not become ruffians
Pick, clean, wash them for thee.

Arrest all those who prostitute
Make them thy own great saints
Force them to preach and not keep mute
To lift each soul that faints.

The 'robbers and kidnappers' gang
All those that ruin the street
Bind them to the cross Jesus hang
Make swift and light their feet.

The heathen land so dark and sick
Where Satan rules like king
Give him on the head just a kick
Tell him you own the ring.

59. Keep Not Thy Blessing Lord on Hold
to the tune of: HOW SWEET THE NAME OF JESUS SOUNDS

Keep not thy blessing lord on hold
Instead let them unfold
Restore to us a thousand times
Whate'er we lost to crimes.

Withdraw from us non-thinking hat
Give us a broken heart
The one that understands thy law
And strives to keep them raw.

Thine is the weak, the faint, the mild
Thine is the rude, and wild
Thine is the slow, the fast, lazy
The mad and the crazy.

Speak dear lord to us, O please speak
And let us reach our peak
Command and calm, redress, restore
Heal our ill-stinking sore.

For foolishness can never win
Unless it rules the bin,
For stupidity cannot thrive
Unless no one, to drive.

60. We Move from Place to Place in Life
to the tune of: HOW SWEET THE NAME OF JESUS SOUNDS

We move from place to place in life
Fighting with stress and strife
We trek, we walk, we crawl, we run
In the rain and the sun.

We cross from sea to sea to live
Facing the storm in five
We starve, we fast, and we longer
Hoping to stop danger.

We fly always from air to air
Wanting life to be fair
We fear, we die, and we wake up
Still hanging far on top.

Dear saviour, hearken to our plea
We call to only thee,
There's none to make us a rich tea
If thou from us do flee.

Be with us, holy God of war
Be with us when we fly,
Be with us when we sail or drive
Lord be with us till dawn.

The hymns in *Chariots of Archangels* may be set to the tunes indicated after each title. The tunes are available in *The Ancient & Modern Hymn Book* and *Ekpere Na Abu (The Igbo Hymn Book)* and elsewhere.

Ngozi Olivia Osuoha

Ngozi Olivia Osuoha is a Nigerian poet, writer and thinker. A graduate of Estate Management with experience in Banking and Broadcasting.

She has thirteen poetry books published in Kenya, Canada, the Philippines, USA, and others. She has also co-authored one (with Kenyan literary critic Amos O. Ojwang').

She has been featured in over sixty-five international anthologies and also has published over two hundred and fifty poems and articles in over twenty countries.

Many of her poems have been translated and published into other languages, including Spanish, Russian, Romanian, Polish, Khloe, Farsi, and Arabic, among others.

She has won many awards; she is a one time *Best of the Net* nominee, and she has numerous words on marble.

www.ingramcontent.com/pod-product-compliance
Lightning Source LLC
Chambersburg PA
CBHW052205110526
44591CB00012B/2088